Reflective Meditations Trilogy:
Understanding My Trauma,
Healing My Trauma,
and
Letting Go–Forgiveness!

Script and photography by
Audrey Tait, MS

Copyright © 2017 by Audrey Tait

Published by Inspirational Insights Counselling, Inc.

All rights reserved

No part of this book may be reproduced, stored in a retrieval system, transmitted in any form or by any means, electronic, photocopying, mechanical, recording, photographing or otherwise, except in the format received, without the written permission of the author and the publisher.

Library and Archives Canada Cataloguing in Publication

Tait, Audrey, 1959-, author, photographer
  Reflective meditations trilogy / script and photography by
  Audrey Tait, MS.

Includes index.
Contents: [Trilogy 1] Understanding my trauma; Healing my trauma; Letting go--forgiveness!
-- [trilogy 2] Understanding my authentic self; Believing in myself; Loving myself; Understanding my boundaries.
Issued in print and electronic formats.
ISBN 978-0-9952326-6-2 (trilogy 1 : softcover)
--ISBN 978-0-9952326-8-6 (trilogy 2 : softcover).
--ISBN 978-0-9952326-7-9 (trilogy 1 : EPUB)
--ISBN 978-0-9952326-9-3 (trilogy 2 : EPUB)

1. Psychic trauma. 2. Self-acceptance. 3. Meditation. I. Title.

BF575.S37T35 2017. 158.1. C2017-903422-7
                                C2017-903423-5

Inspirational Insights Counselling, Inc.
Red Deer, Alberta Canada
www.inspirationalinsightscounselling.com

Dedication

Dedicated to all those who read this book and seriously search to heal from their own trauma!

How to Use the Books

Each book is set up in sixty short thoughts that can be used as a daily reflective meditation. Take the time to read what it says and think about it throughout the day. You can ask yourself the questions "How does this relate to me?" "What can I learn from it?" "What can I do differently?" and "Did that work for me or do I need to change something else?"

Book Contents

Reflective Meditations Trilogy:
1. Understanding My Trauma
Page 1
2. Healing My Trauma
Page 45
3. Letting Go–Forgiveness
Page 95
4. Further Reading
Page 139
5. About the Author
Page 140

Contents

1. Introduction.....3
2. What Is Trauma?.....4
3. Understanding Trauma.....6
4. Understanding the Flight Response to Trauma.....12
5. Understanding the Fight Response to Trauma.....17
6. Understanding the Freeze Response to Trauma.....22
7. Understanding the Submit Response to Trauma.....26
8. Understanding the Cry Response to Trauma.....29
9. Understanding Relational Trauma.....32
10. Trauma and Neurochemistry.....36
11. Healing Trauma.....39
12. Understanding Healing.....43

Introduction

You may come to a time in life when you realize that you do not really understand the trauma in your life or how it has affected you. Trauma can be a onetime event or chronic over time. It can be simple or complex. It affects everyone differently— some not at all and others more distressingly. When we react to events in our lives, we have to cope with the reality of trauma. A lot of times that coping is something that we need to continue for life and we do not realize the trauma is still affecting us. We do not realize we do things that are a reaction to the trauma from the past. This book is about unraveling our reaction to past trauma so that we can understand our behavior and change it.

What Is Trauma?

Day 1 Trauma—such a horrible thing

She sat on the closed-door trap—just doing as he told her. "Do this," "Do that," "Now, do this," and so it went while she was wondering what was happening to her. This may be something that has happened to you. Physical assault with no way of escape—perhaps it was something during military service—or a terrifying car accident. These are some of the many examples of past trauma that may be haunting our lives.

Day 2 My trauma is never my fault

Trauma is never the fault of the victim. Let us say that together, BEING TRAUMATIZED IS NEVER MY FAULT. I

DID NOT CAUSE IT. I AM NOT RESPONSIBLE FOR IT. I DID NOT CHOOSE IT. AND AGAIN, I WILL SAY BEING TRAUMATIZED IS NOT MY FAULT! This is something to remember for the rest of my life. I will write it down and put it in a safe place where I can see this reminder daily. Even if my behavior has traumatized other people, I more than likely have been traumatized myself. I still need to say this to myself, write it down, and put it where I will see it.

Day 3 Our journey

Come with me on this journey as we unravel our trauma from the past, learn how we continue to play out the trauma without even knowing it, and start to learn how to change things and learn to be a calmer person, so we can have more peace, love, joy, and serenity in life. We will take a look at different types of reactions to trauma, gain a better idea of how we reacted to trauma, and learn what we can do to change that reaction. It will be a difficult journey, yet one of the most rewarding journeys of our life. Have the courage to come with me.

Understanding Trauma

Day 4 Types of trauma

Different people react to what happens in their life differently. What is traumatizing to one person may not be trauma to another person. Some people react to trauma immediately, while others may not react for months or even years. Trauma comes in many different forms. Trauma may be a onetime event or it may be chronic over time. It may be simple or complex.

Day 5 Overt versus covert

Trauma may be overt (obvious), such as a serious car accident, military service, childhood abuse, or sexual assault. It may be more covert (subtle), such as manipulation and control. When it is covert, it is harder to see and understand; yet, it will still leave you feeling that all is not well with your soul.

Day 6 Whose fault?

Trauma is never the fault of the victim. I will say it again, "TRAUMA IS NEVER THE FAULT OF THE VICTIM." You do not need to blame yourself for the trauma, especially if you were a child when the trauma happened. Your job now is to understand the trauma, deal with the trauma, and move past it to get on with your life—to find a life that is satisfying and filled with a lot of peace, joy, serenity, and hope. This is the long-term goal that you are looking for.

Day 7 Trauma bonds

Bonds that are formed in trauma are stronger than in normal healthy relations. This explains why it is hard for someone to leave a spouse who continues to be abusive. It also helps explain why it is so hard for a child to tell a trusted adult what another person is doing to them. If this has been your issue, you need to find someone you can trust to talk to. You may need to find a therapist who can help you, someone who can help you learn to say "no" to the abuser or help you find another place to live for as long as needed in order to break the cycle.

Day 8 Emotional responses to trauma

It is usually the strong emotional reactions to trauma that people have a hard time dealing with. These are the emotions that will not go away and need to be dealt with. Usually they will drive us to do one of two things—either they push us over the top or make us go numb. Strong emotions take us into flight, flight, or rage, whereas numbing emotions take us into freeze and submit. These are two opposite extremes and in the middle are normal emotions—living life, having conversations, working, enjoying experiences with friends and family members where there is respect between all engaged.

Day 9 Boundary breaking in trauma

In trauma, there is a breaking of boundaries. Some boundaries are obvious, like when someone invades my physical space, whether it is them standing too close to me or physical or sexual assault. Broken verbal boundaries are harder to see—sometimes it is not until later that it becomes clear that someone was trying to manipulate or control you. In a trauma bond, this is really hard to see. Then, there is the person who lies a lot (such as when your partner is having a relationship with another person) and you may not be aware of this. If your gut does not trust what is going on, then it is time to really take a good look at what is happening. Start asking the questions about what does not make sense. During this process, keep yourself safe—you may need a therapist or trusted friend to help you.

Day 10 How we react to trauma

There are a number of ways we can respond to trauma. It is like coming across a bear. What would you do? Take flight, fight, freeze, or submit? Somewhere in all of that, you might scream and the aftermath would lead to recuperation. This is very much the animal response we have in our bodies as humans.

Inevitably, after trauma, we get stuck in one or more of these responses and it becomes a way of life for us that we are not even aware of. The next time your emotions get intense or you do not feel like doing anything, seriously consider whether this is a response to past trauma. You might notice over time what ways you respond and how they relate to the reactions of trauma that we will look at in the next number of weeks.

Day 11 Reward/reinforcement pathway

Everyone wants to feel good in life. This desire comes from what is called the reward/reinforcement pathway in the brain. When we are not able to feel good due to poor attachment in the past, we may have a lot of negative self-talk, like "I am worthless," "I am helpless," and "I am unlovable." A lot of negative emotions develop. We must find a way to deal with these strong emotions. Sometimes we stuff them down by becoming numb or develop addictions as we try to deal with them. These are unhealthy reactions to trauma.

Day 12 Types of response to trauma

In the next few days and weeks, we will look at the flight response, fight response, freeze response, submit, and attachment cry responses to trauma. Taking a good look at what types of response(s) you had, what types of response(s) you are using in your daily life (perhaps without being aware of it), and what you can do to change this is all part of unraveling your trauma.

Understanding the Flight Response to Trauma

Day 13 Flight

Flight is one way to deal with trauma from the past. The emotional pain is so intolerable that covering it up is the only way to deal with it. One way to cover it up and flee from it is to develop addictions. The more traumas there are—the more to cover up—the more addictions. Addictions may go beyond the typical alcohol and substance use, and include process addictions, compulsive attachments, and addictive feelings. An addiction is something you cannot stop and you need more of over time to achieve the same effect.

Day 14 Substance addictions

Substance addictions include the compulsive use of alcohol, cocaine, methamphetamines, and many other drugs. They enter the body through various methods and some cross the blood/brain barrier to enter the brain. Each drug has a different effect on the brain; yet, the end goal of using is always to dull the senses and forget the pain. This may be what I have done in the past and now I want to change the way I do things.

Day 15 Process addictions

While process addictions do not involve using substances, they are just as addictive as substance addictions. They include sex, food, gambling, work, Internet, and money disorders. Process addictions affect the brain in much the same way that addictive substances do. For example, research is starting to show that the brain of someone addicted to food is affected like that of someone addicted to a substance. If any of these are my issues, I choose to start making changes today.

Day 16 Compulsive attachment

Compulsive attachment at first does not seem like an addiction—it is not something that one would normally consider an addiction. Compulsive attachments include staying with unhealthy people, trauma bonds, codependency, co-addictions, rescuing others, giving too much, managing impressions (what others think about me), and other similar bonds. This is where I lose myself and give to others all the time. In reality, I do not know who I really am deep inside of me: "What are my likes?" "What are my wants?" "What do I really like to do?" and "Who am I?"

Day 17 Feelings

Feelings are what people are fleeing from when it comes to addictions, yet some people are addicted to certain feelings. They seemingly cannot function without strong emotions. They become addicted to the rush that comes with feelings and will create a scene in order to feel that way. They might be addicted to feelings of rage, intensity, fear, love, or self-hatred. So, it is good to remember that some people will always be hard to deal with and interacting with them will leave you feeling traumatized again. On the other hand, you could be the one making someone's life really miserable.

Day 18 How to change

Addictions happen when the line has been crossed from something being optional to no longer being a choice—it takes over one's life. Stopping is not possible on your own. Either you have to hit bottom and come to your senses that you need help or someone does an intervention for you, informing you of the problem and providing consequences if you do not enter treatment. If you are reading this and realize that you have an addiction issue, seek treatment immediately. It will be the best thing you ever did for yourself. While getting help, make sure you deal with the trauma; doing so will decrease your desire to cope by using an addiction.

Day 19 Where to go from here

Addictions are hard to change! It takes persistence and hard work. Certainly, having treatment and support is essential. The support needs to be long term—at least three to five years. Treatment is not just about stopping the addiction—treatment includes the long-term goal of being able to live a normal, healthy life in all areas. It is learning to treat myself and others with respect. It includes learning to have peaceful serenity in my life day after day.

Understanding the Fight Response to Trauma

Day 20 Fight

Fight is one of the active responses to trauma. This may be accomplished in many ways. It might be fighting that is verbal or physical. This could also turn into abusive situations—a wife or child being battered. Fight can be outward aggression, inward aggression, self-harm, or suicide.

Day 21 Outward aggression

Outward aggression is what hurts others. It is the rage, the verbal abuse, the physical abuse—battering—the mental abuse ("You cannot do that"), the sexual abuse, such as sexual assault and rape. Also, there is manipulation and control or passive-aggressive behavior that dominates others so that they cannot grow and change. This becomes a release so that you, the perpetrator, feel better—a releasing of your strong emotions. The worst is the rage and premeditation of wanting someone gone—killed. This is serious stuff. There are better ways to cope that need to be learned. Deep breathing is just a beginning and something that you can start practicing right now.

Day 22 Inward aggression

Inward aggression is taking the fight inside of you. This is aggression to the self, and it can take many different forms—from the physical to the mental to the social to the sexual to the spiritual. It can be overdoing something or not doing enough of it. This interrupts the balance that is needed in life. Having one piece of pie for dessert is normal and balanced—eating a whole pie at once, especially if hiding the knowledge of it from others, would be an example of having too much. Exercising too little or too much would be another example. The idea is to find balance in life.

Day 23 Self-harm

Self-harm is an inward aggression. Self-harm can be the more obvious forms of self-cutting and self-spanking. It can also take on the less obvious forms of not taking care of oneself (not eating healthily, not exercising enough, not maintaining ideal body weight, not accepting your body image, listening to lies of others, not loving yourself, and many other things). It could be not taking the medications you need to be healthy or that a health care provider has recommended. In the end, it is only me who is hurt by this. Instead of the abused being hurt by others, the abused is hurt by themselves—and thus the person stays in the victim mode. I choose to stop self-harm behavior starting right now.

Day 24 Suicide

Suicide is the extreme form of inward aggression. It is when someone has been hurt and traumatized so much that they do not want to live anymore. They are not able to deal with the strong emotional reactions to life or they are so numbed out that life seems worthless. Nobody deserves this kind of pain. If this is you, seek help today; if you cannot find a therapist to help you, go to your local emergency department. Everyone is valuable and can find purpose and meaning. Do not let what others say about you affect who you are and prevent you from finding your purpose in life. If you have been unable to find your purpose by yourself, seek others who can help you.

Day 25 How to change

To change takes time. There needs to be boundaries—in this case, boundaries with the self—a foreign concept for a lot of people, especially for those who come from rigid religious environments. Life is about loving ourselves in a healthy way, so we can love others from a place of being able to give without expecting anything in return (if I do something for you, then I expect you to give back to me). The boundaries with self are about what I will and will not do—and who I will get to help me, a safe person such as a therapist.

Day 26 Where to go from here

Where I go from here depends on me—what do I need to change first? If I am suicidal, then I need to seek immediate attention. I need people who can help keep me safe from myself. If I am at the point where my anger is out of control and I will hurt someone else, then I need immediate assistance to protect another person. In both cases, the best help is at the emergency department of the local hospital. If this is not my issue, then I need to seek help to change the behaviors that are slowly eroding who I am and who I want to be.

Understanding the Freeze Response to Trauma

Day 27 Freeze

Freeze is another animal response to trauma, another way that one reacts to trauma. In the freeze response, one cannot move. A lot of times this may come after fight or flight and before submit. There may be fear, terror, anxiety, or a similar type of response. This may come after trying to flee or take flight. It may be what one feels after the trauma has passed in the immediate time until the heart calms down.

Day 28 Anxiety

Anxiety can happen in the moment of the trauma and it can be a response that is carried for life. Every time there is a similar situation, such as seeing a snake or a thunderstorm or something else that triggers memories from the past event, the anxiety returns. The body reacts in a way similar to the trauma. Unless treated, this will continue for the long term. Gradual exposure with help is one way to treat this.

Day 29 Fear

Fear is more than anxiety. It can be a feeling that happens in the moment or it can be thoughts that we allow to dominate our minds—thoughts of what may happen in the near or far future, what may or may not come to pass. It may be that the feared event never happened; we just thought it would. This take up a lot of our mental energy and keeps us from peace and serenity. Fear is the opposite of love. Fear does not allow love to surface—to be connected with ourself and others.

Day 30 Terror

Terror is extreme fear—in the moment. It's hard to describe this feeling with words unless you have felt it. If this is bringing up strong emotions and body sensations for you, take a deep breath from the diaphragm. Doing so will help you calm down. Deep breathing is something to practice all the time to help yourself stay calm.

Day 31 How to change

Change comes slowly with intentional exposure to whatever we find terrifying, whether it's life events, snakes, or thunderstorms. Of course, if the freeze reaction comes from sexual abuse, then exposure is not appropriate. Healing takes time—it is like opening a scary door a little the first time and then, when one has had enough, closing the door. Another time the door may remain open a little longer. Maybe the next time opening the same door is not safe. This is a boundary that can be flexible and changed as needed. Slowly, the anxiety, fear, and terror will decrease.

*Day 32 **Where to go from here***

When it comes to thoughts of fear, one can simply decide not to listen to those thoughts. It is helpful to focus on how unrealistic those thoughts are and then decide to change what one is thinking about. Completely healing from anxiety, fear, and terror may require help from a trusted friend who will not be critical or make one feel horrible. Friends can help with different levels of exposure to the feared item. If they are not able to help or are unhelpful, then it might be necessary to find professional help.

Understanding the Submit Response to Trauma

Day 33 Submit

Many times, after trying to get out of a traumatic situation, the only thing left is to submit. Certainly, a child who is being abused by a bigger person would have no way to escape. This could also be the case in sexual assault or with trauma that occurred in the military. The best thing to do in such situations is to submit. In the aftermath, this can bring collapse and depression.

Day 34 Collapse

Collapse is about not having the energy to cope with what is going on around us. In a way, it is about avoiding our daily surroundings. This can also happen after the death of a loved one. It can be especially hard around the holidays or when by oneself.

Day 35 Depression

Depression is deeper than a collapse. It is not sleeping properly—waking up at any time of the night. It is eating too much or too little. It is feeling tired all the time, even to the point of not getting out of bed or taking a shower. This all results from feelings that are very negative.

Day 36 How to change

This is one area where it is helpful to change one's thoughts—changing the negative to something positive. When I do not feel like doing something, I can say to myself, "I will do this for just five minutes." Then after five minutes, I can tell myself, "That was not so bad; I can do it for ten more minutes." And slowly change will come—one step at a time.

Day 37 What to do from here

If you are not able to start the change process one step at a time, then it is best to seek help. You may start with self-help books and talking to a safe person. If this is not enough, then seek help from a physician or therapist. I may need long-term help to get me going so that I can continue to make healthy changes in my life.

Understanding the Cry Response to Trauma

Day 38 Attachment cry

When babies have a need that is not being met, the only way they have to respond is the attachment cry. If no one comes after hearing their cries, then they eventually will stop crying and learn that their needs are not important. When needs are not met on a consistent basis, they grow to learn not to state their needs and eventually feel that they have no needs. It is not worth asking, as they will not have their need met. Basic needs are food, water, sleep, shelter, warmth, health care, and protection. These are needed by everyone regardless of their age or living situation.

Day 39 Sound alarm

In nature, there are times in the middle of the night and even during the day when you will hear the bloodcurdling scream of the adult animal. It sends shivers down one's spine. As adults, we at times are surprised by someone who scares us and the natural reaction is to scream. Some medical procedures will produce the same effect as a scream. One of the ways to be stuck in the attachment cry is to always be sounding the alarm. If a person does not like what is happening to them, they can scream at the other people around.

Day 40 Crying

There are times in life when crying is expected and the tears need to be released in a healthy way. Grief is one such time. It could be a simple grief in not being able to do something. It could be the loss of physical ability as one grows older, and it could be the loss of a loved one through divorce or death. Also, culture often dictates how and when we cry. What is needed is to have a healthy balance with crying—not to be a constant screamer and not to never cry.

Day 41 How to change

Change starts with realizing that there is a problem. People do not like to be yelled at. Being scared and yelling is one thing. Yelling to get your own way is a form of manipulation and trying to control the situation. This takes time to change. It takes patience. Counting to ten when you do not like what is happening is one way to slow down your reaction, so you have time to think about not screaming.

Day 42 What to do from here

Practice, practice, practice! If this is an issue for you and practice does not help, then you need to seek professional help. It may make the difference between having friends who choose to be around you and having family and friends who do not want to be around you.

Understanding Relational Trauma

Day 43 Relational trauma

Relationship trauma is trauma that happens between two individuals. This can happen anytime during a life but especially early in life. It has a lot to do with the relationship between the primary caregiver and the infant. It can be a secure relationship or not secure relationship. This relationship from the past has a lot to do with how we relate to others in our current life. How we related in early life is more than likely how we relate in our current life—in our marriages especially.

Day 44 Secure attachment

A secure relationship means we are able to relate to others without yelling, screaming, manipulating, controlling, freezing, fighting—inward or outward—or fleeing. A secure attachment is two healthy individuals coming together to relate in a meaningful way. This might include sitting down and having coffee together, just gazing into each other's eyes and feeling deep contentment, or having a deep conversation knowing that you are being accepted for who you are.

Day 45 Avoidant attachment

Insecure attachments could be avoidant relationships if you just avoid the other person. This behavior could be healthy if it's about creating a boundary to protect yourself. If this boundary is not intentional, then it could be unhealthy and a pattern that needs to change. It might be a pattern that you developed early in life, perhaps before you could even talk. This will take some work to change.

Day 46 Ambivalent attachment

Insecure attachments could also be ambivalent. This is where you do not really care about how the relationship goes. It could go either way—moving into a deepening friendship or fading away. You do not feel like putting the effort into it and do not care what happens. This is where choosing and being intentional about relationships helps.

Day 47 Disorganized

Insecure attachments can be disorganized. In this type of attachment, you do not know what to expect from the other person. It can be really hard to deal with. Should I approach the other person—will I be accepted or will I be rejected? This not knowing can cause one to be very shy. A certain amount of anxiety needs to be overcome or ignored to approach another person in uncomfortable situations. This takes practice. Asking questions before going to a new event will help decrease the anxiety.

Day 48 Where to go from here

Attachments are meant to be secure. In adulthood, one can earn a secure attachment. It takes work and effort. The first secure attachment must be with yourself. Being able to be alone with yourself and comfortable with it provides peace and serenity. The idea is to be able to stop negative thoughts like "I am no good" and replace them with something positive. This is the goal because then it will be easier to be around other people. It is also good to create boundaries with people who do not allow you to feel peace and serenity around them or people you do not feel secure around.

Trauma and Neurochemistry

Day 49 Neuropathways

Trauma affects the brain, including the neuropathways in the brain. We used the best coping method we could at the time of the trauma and our coping created certain neuropathways that have stayed in place. There has been no reason to change and more than likely there has been no desire to change. In fact, many people can become addicted to having chaos in their life. They will make chaos if there is none. This just keeps the neuropathways functioning in the same way. To change them takes time, persistence, and patience.

Day 50 Change

What worked in the past does not necessarily work today. Getting angry, freezing, avoiding, fleeing, or crying at your boss, partner, children, or friends can have devastating consequences. It breaks relationships. Now is the time to think about changing the neuropathways in my brain. Deciding to become assertive instead of using unhealthy ways of coping is a step in the right direction.

Day 51 Being assertive

Becoming assertive means being able to ask for what I need (without anger, control, and manipulation) and still allow the other person to say "yes" or "no." It does not mean the other person has to fulfill my needs. It means I have permission to ask and he or she has permission to say no. It means I do not do this to take advantage of another person. It allows for an equal give-and-take in a relationship. If one needs to set boundaries, then it is a matter of stating what I will not tolerate and what I will do if the problem continues. It also means that when I state my boundaries, I am willing to do what I say I will do. This is still a form of being assertive.

Healing Trauma

Day 52 How do I currently respond to trauma?

It is interesting to see the different types of trauma and how they can affect people. The healing begins when I take a serious look at how I respond to difficult situations in my life. Do I still fight, flight, freeze, submit, or cry? The next time I feel my emotions rising or falling (numbing), I may want to ask myself, "Am I responding in a way related to a past trauma?" I may not be able to do this in the moment; however, afterward I will take the time to think about it and how I could have done things differently.

Day 53 What is my pattern?

As I begin to see the pattern of how I respond and see how I am stuck in that pattern, I can begin to try to change how I do things. This is not always easy. I may need to be able to speak up for myself, or I may need to be able to calm myself down. Either way, I can take a deep breath from my diaphragm, slowly release it, and calmly say what I need to say. If this is really hard for me, then I can find a safe person (someone who will not tell others)—a friend or therapist—who can help me practice this.

Day 54 Change

The pattern of trauma that I have continued over the years is what I have learned. It may very well have been the best thing for me in the moment. If I did not act that way at the time, then things could have been worse for me in the moment. Now, when I am not in a trauma situation and I start to react the same way, this is not healthy for me. So, now that I have an idea of how I react, I can start to do things differently. The next step is learning how I can react differently—this may take some thinking. Certainly, the idea is to find a way to react in a calm manner.

Day 55 Practice

After finding and deciding a different way to deal with my traumatic reactions, then it is time to practice it with a safe person. This could be a trusted friend or a therapist. If this is not possible, then I could write out a response and practice saying it in front of the mirror many, many times. This would help to right the old tapes of how I responded to trauma and would mean that next time I would be more prepared to try my new behavior.

Day 56 Reflecting

If this change has not worked for me, then I need to start again and find a new solution to the problem—my old behavior that I need to change. Again, I would need to practice this ahead of time to ensure that I am likely to change. If this does not work, then I will need to try another strategy to change my behavior. At some point, if things do not work and the other person continues to not respect my requests and me, then I may need to take a time-out. This is certainly okay if I am willing to return to the discussion later. After making so many attempts to change, it might be time to consider if this is a good relationship for me.

Day 57 Safety

If there is any abuse happening to me, it is my right and duty to remove myself and any dependents from that situation as soon as possible. Never, in changing my behavior and how I react, should I allow others to verbally, physically, or sexually abuse me. Neither should spiritual and religious abuse ever be allowed. Safety is my number one priority.

Day 58 Healing

In the end, the idea of healing trauma is to be able to escape the rut of how I was coping so that I can move on—so that I can learn to be a calm person where my emotions do not drive me to do things I do not want to do. So that I do not fight, flight, freeze, submit, or behave in any other negative way in response to overly stimulating situations. The other idea is to set boundaries around myself to manage situations so that they are not overly stimulating for me. This will take a lot of practice.

Understanding Healing

Day 59 Where to go from here

This has been an intense journey through a very difficult subject—unraveling my own trauma. It never is an easy subject to deal with. In reality, it is easier not to have to deal with it. Through this journey, we have looked at how trauma affects people in different ways. Then each one of us has looked specifically at how it has affected us. Knowing how it has affected me helps me understand what I need to change. Defining the problem is always helpful in changing it, because from here one can make choices on how to change and if it does not work, then trying something different is the way to go.

Day 60 New beginnings

This is the beginning of an awesome journey —a journey that will make me a better person deep inside myself and within deep relationships that I pursue in life. May you always continue on this healing journey. As life becomes calmer every day with more and more peace, love, joy, and serenity in my life, it will become more meaningful and purposeful.

You can do it!

Keep up the good work!

Contents

1. Introduction.....47
2. Healing Trauma.....48
3. Healing in the Moment.....51
4. Dealing with Strong Emotions.....55
5. Dealing with Numbing Emotions.....60
6. Healing Specific Types of Traumas.....64
7. Healing Relational Trauma.....71
8. Boundaries Around Trauma.....75
9. Boundaries of Forgiveness (Letting Go).....80
10. Ways to Help Diminish or Prevent Trauma..... 86
11. Conclusion.....93

Introduction

Healing one's trauma is a lifelong journey. A lot of the time it does not seem like an adventure; the hurt, pain, strong emotions, or numbing emotions can be overwhelming. I, as the author, know what it is like. I know that a healing journey comes with all these emotions. I also know that, in the end and as the journey progresses, more and more often there are times of peace, joy, serenity, and happiness. It is these emotions that are the goal of this journey.

Come with me on this journey; I'll take you through the path that I took during my own healing, while reaching out to guide you on your individual journey. As we go, I suggest that you take one day at a time, read the thought, and meditate upon it throughout the day. Decide what you can learn from it and then take the time to make any necessary changes. If you have been on this journey for a while, know that there is still valuable information and techniques that you can gain and use. If, on the other hand, you are just getting started on your journey from trauma, be patient with yourself. There will be a lot to take in and learn.

Healing Trauma

Day 1 Trauma

Trauma comes in many forms. The most obvious are the major forms of trauma: natural disaster, wars, car accidents, sexual assault, physical abuse, verbal abuse, and others. Then there are the smaller types of trauma that, while not life altering, may nonetheless be frustrating. We may feel this way, for example, when others attempt to control and manipulate us. Chronic trauma is another type of trauma that we may not notice or be concerned with at first, but after repetition for years, the harmful effects can add up.

Day 2 First step

The first step in healing from trauma is to simply decide to move toward healing. This may begin with a step to come out of the denial of what happened; to stop keeping the secrets of your family and others; to have a desire to change your life; to go through the process of healing and learning how to do things differently; and to find a safe place and safe people to do this with. If this is your choice, then I invite you to come with me on this journey.

Day 3 The journey

On this journey, we will look at different types of healing, different healing responses to trauma, the importance of setting boundaries around trauma and forgiveness, and proactive ways to prevent or diminish trauma in the future. These are steps and tools that I have found helpful in this healing process. You may still want to have professional help along the way.

Healing in the Moment

Day 4 Where to begin

Healing trauma takes time and effort. The process is not always easy; it requires understanding what happened and then managing and healing from it. This book is also available in other countries from Amazon. This book will continue where the last book left off—taking the next step to begin healing trauma.

Day 5 The size of trauma

Hardly a person has ever lived who has not experienced some kind of trauma. It may be the small disappointments that happen when an event(s) was canceled or it may be the more difficult trauma of a serious car accident, military service, rape, or natural disaster. These events produce a traumatic reaction in some people, and this needs to be dealt with. Hiding trauma keeps the wounds open and fresh, ready to be re-experienced at any time. Working through the healing process allows the scars to heal. Although the scars will never fade entirely, in time they will be barely noticeable. The emotions around the scars will also diminish. This is the goal of healing trauma—to decrease the emotional scars. Today, I will consider some of my scars.

Day 6 Emotional scars

You might have a number of emotional scars that need to be healed. Depending on where you look, you can find a list of different emotions. Some of the basic emotions are sadness, joy, fear, and anger. For now, let's work at identifying and naming your emotions. This is easy for some and extremely hard for others. Emotions are a right-brain function, and this may be something that has been shut down for you due to trauma. Learning to name emotions is a way to begin the healing process. Even being numb is an emotion. Today, I will try to name three emotions.

Day 7 Emotional reactions

My emotional reactions come from my cognitions, or thoughts, around an event. If you view an event as pleasant, then you will feel happy about it. If you view it as negative, then you may have some strong emotions or numbing emotions about the event. If you stop and take a serious look at the event and view it from different perspectives, then your emotional reaction(s) could change. Today, when I react to something strongly, I will take another look from all of the perspectives to see if I can change my thinking and emotions.

Day 8 Two ways to deal with trauma

People deal with trauma in different ways—some deal with it on their own, and others turn to others for help. Then, there is the combination of the two—dealing with it by oneself and with others. Today, I will observe my reactions to see how I deal with the disappointments that I face.

Day 9 My choice of the journey

Dealing with strong or numbing emotions is one of the first steps in healing trauma. If you cannot talk about the trauma because of the emotions, then you need to deal with the emotions—to be able to control the emotions. Being angry with another person hurts all involved in the issue. Taking that strong emotional reaction to what happens in life inward—stuffing it down, numbing it —only hurts you and helps you lose your sense of well-being and who you are deep inside. This is what leads to depression. Today, I will choose the healing process as I learn to deal with my emotions.

Dealing with Strong Emotions

Day 10 Meaning with strong emotion

Strong emotions come from a number of places. Anger comes from broken boundaries. Grief comes from loss. Strong emotions usually come from the fight-or-flight response to trauma. Regardless of the emotions, when they are strong and override the functioning areas of the brain, something needs to be done to bring the emotions under your self-control. This is not always easy. A good cry may release some of the emotions in the moment; however, if the emotions are not dealt with, they will come back to haunt you. Following are some ways to deal with those deep emotions. Today, I will watch for strong emotions that I need to deal with.

Day 11 Deep breathing

Deep breathing is a great way to calm your body system. Maybe you have heard of it before and tried it but it did not work for you. Well, breathing deeply is only part of what needs to be done. If you are a singer, you will know what it means to breathe deeply from the diaphragm (the area around the belly button). Here you want your diaphragm to fill with air. You could place your hands over or around your belly button to feel the air entering and leaving your diaphragm. The lungs must not be moving, the rib cage must be still, and the shoulders must not rise. This is the breathing that calms the body down. People with a history of numerous traumas have learned to breathe through their lungs with shallow breaths. Today, I will practice breathing through my diaphragm—watching my belly rise!

Day 12 Posture for deep breathing

Another very important part of deep breathing is your posture. When you are stooped over or collapsed in the chest, it is really hard to breathe well. Other body postures also make it difficult to breathe properly. You need to practice sitting, standing, walking, and lying down with a correct posture. Envision having a string attached to the top of your head pulling gently upward so your body moves into correct alignment. If this is really difficult for you, your muscles may have become so used to your current posture that it will take more effort to change. Seeking physical therapy may be helpful in correcting your posture. Today, I will practice correct posture.

Day 13 Grounding

Another way to calm your body system down is to do what's called grounding. This means physically feeling your feet on the floor, your thighs on the seat of your chair, and your back against the back of the chair. Grounding is a real physical sensation. Another part of grounding involves looking around the room and naming whatever you see that is interesting. This ensures that your mind is where you are physically. It prevents dissociation or a separation of mind and body. Today, I will practice grounding.

Day 14 Lying down

When all else fails to calm down your system —deep breathing, straight posture, and grounding—then you can lie down on your stomach. In this position, deep breathing comes automatically. This is not something you can do in every situation, and for this reason it may be a last resort for calming down. When I go to bed tonight, I will lie on my stomach and see if the deep breathing comes. I will also focus on what it feels like so that when I try deep breathing while standing, sitting, and walking, I will know what to expect.

Day 15 Counting

When you are someplace away from home and have strong emotions, you can try counting to ten in your thoughts. This may seem like a senseless thing to do, but it gives your "thinking brain" time to function so you can make a rational decision. What happens with strong emotions is that parts of the brain stop functioning, making it impossible for the thinking part of the brain to work. If this happens, you may do something that you will regret later and then have to live with the consequences. Today, I will practice counting to ten out loud or in my mind, depending on where I am.

Day 16 Standing

If you cannot get the thinking brain on board, then try standing up to help the thinking brain into action. This is a very useful tactic. If you are in a situation that feels overwhelming, simply get up and walk around. Excuse yourself and go get a cup of water, visit the bathroom, or take a short walk. This type of activity will clear the air and help you think better. It might also give others around you time to think. Today, I will practice standing when my emotions start to become strong.

Day 17 Continue practicing

When strong emotions come, they need to be dealt with in the moment. In a sense, it could be a matter of life or death. In a traumatic event that is currently happening, any thinking is better than not thinking at all. Taking action right away may enable you to make the next decision that will get you out of the situation, if possible. Today, I will continue to practice dealing with strong emotions.

Dealing with Numbing Emotions

Day 18 Calm emotions

In between strong emotions and numbing emotions are calm emotions. This is where you want your emotions to be. This is where you find peace, happiness, love, joy, serenity, and many other awesome emotions. Achieving this goal of being with your emotions takes a maturity of character that comes over time. When you were traumatized, your emotions were hijacked. Living more in this area of contentment is the goal in life. Today, I will practice having serenity in my life.

Day 19 Numbing emotions

At other times the emotions go the opposite way. You become so numb that you do not feel like moving and life is hard to engage in. This is very much like freeze-and-submit responses to trauma in animals and ourselves. When the trauma occurred, this may have been the best way to respond. Now it does not work. Being disengaged, or somehow separated, from everyday life brings unwanted consequences. It needs to be changed. Freeze-and-submit can be where fear, despondency, and depression come from. Depression is repressed anger turned inward due to a boundary violation. Today, I will notice when I do not feel like doing anything.

Day 20 A different kind of breathing

When you are feeling down and need to increase your energy level, it is helpful to breathe from deep in the lungs. As you practice this, you should be able to see your rib cage move in and out on all sides of your body. This will help bring up your energy level. You might want to put your hands on the sides of your rib cage so that you can feel your ribs move in and out with your breathing. After such lung breathing, you will feel more like doing the things that need to be done. The next time I do not feel like doing anything, I will try breathing from deep in my lungs.

Day 21 A story

Recently, I was sitting in a meeting where the topic turned to something that was very emotional for me—and the heaving, crying, and moaning sounds wanted to start. I said to myself, "I can deal with this later." Then, I straightened my posture, let my body automatically do deep breathing, and concentrated my focus on something else. Hours later, I allowed myself to go through the emotions that had tried to sideline me in the meeting. Other times, when appropriate, I will deal with the emotions in the moment.

Day 22 Numb emotions to strong emotions

Going from numbing emotions to strong emotions can happen in a moment. This means going from being passive to possibly being aggressive or having other strong emotions. When this happens, you will need to change what you do to calm your system down. Begin by changing the type of breathing you're doing—going from lung breathing to diaphragm breathing. If this still does not work, then you can stand up or lie down. Today, I will practice alternating breathing from my lungs to my diaphragm or from my diaphragm to my lungs.

Healing Specific Types of Traumas

Day 23 Types of trauma responses

We are like the animals in our responses to trauma; we fight, flight, freeze, and submit. These responses can get stuck at the time of the trauma, and then we tend to repeat these responses when similar situations come up in life. For example, if we were able to fight at the time of the trauma, we will continue to fight with people who break our boundaries (whether the boundaries are obvious or unstated or unknown)—this leads to those who bully. It could also be inward fighting with yourself—self-harm. Flight is leaving the scene of action(s)—being avoidant of what happens in life—not being able to complete a project when the going gets tough. The freeze response is stopping in the middle of what is happening and not being able to deal with it. The submit response means submitting, or giving in, to what others want you to do, like in childhood molestation. Do you remember from Reflective Meditations: Unraveling My Trauma *what your response to trauma was?*

At the time of the trauma, there may have been no other way to react. Certainly, for an infant there is no other option but to submit and cry. But later, there is the possibility to heal and adapt to a healthier life. These responses to trauma come from the lower part of the brain, and healing needs to engage the upper areas of the brain. It reality, this means making new connections of the neurons as new behavior emerges. This is a process that takes time. One day at a time—one decision at a time. Am I willing to start the process of change?

It is quite possible that you may have more than one response to trauma. You may respond to one person the same way all of the time and to another person in a totally different way. Somewhere between the active responses of fight/flight and the inactive responses of freeze/submit is a healthy way to live—not over-reactive and not under-reactive—being engaged in everyday life with a peace and serenity that comes with healing. This takes time to develop.

Day 24 Healing the fight response

To heal the fight response to trauma, you first need to understand what the problem is. Fight includes physical fights, such as bullying, wife battering, grabbing, hitting, punching, kicking; and intellectual fights, including put-downs and negative talk, such as "You cannot do this or that." This is the outward fight toward others. Then there is the inward fight—self-harm, self-hurting (cutting, etc.)—along with negative self-talk. The ultimate self-harm is suicide. Breathing and grounding from earlier practices is the place to start when I want to stop hurting others or myself. Transforming negative self-talk into positive self-talk is another change—saying, "I am worthwhile, I am helpful, and I am lovable," is a place to start. This is changing the beliefs at the very core of my being. Today, I will practice changing my negative self-talk to positive self-talk.

Day 25 Healing the flight response

Healing the flight response to trauma also requires understanding what is happening. Flight means leaving the scene, avoiding the problem, not talking about what is the obvious, avoiding the addict's continual abuse, not paying the bills, not taking responsibility for one's life, neglecting what life requires of you, not working, and not taking care of your responsibilities at home. The way to make changes is to start to take responsibility for yourself. Learn what you must do to look after yourself. Then, begin learning to take care of those who are dependent on you. Start one day at a time to make small changes. Your brain will respond by making changes and it will get easier each day. Today, I choose to make changes to my life, to improve my life, and to be responsible for myself.

Day 26 Healing the freeze response

Healing from the freeze response again starts with understanding the process. To have a freeze response means that you freeze in the moment: having fear; not being able to function; freezing on stage when you need to perform or give a speech; or freezing in the moment of conflict, not being able to respond. During these times, it is good to take a deep breath from the lungs—to boost your energy level so that you can engage in the moment and respond to the situation in a way that is appropriate. If this is an issue for you, go back and practice deep breathing from your lungs. Practice correct posture so that when the freeze response happens, your body will automatically do this type of breathing. I will make positive changes in my life today.

Day 27 Healing the submit response

Healing the submit response starts with understanding what you are submitting to or allowing. You have to take a deeper look at what is going on around you. As an infant or child, you may have had no choice but to submit to what others did or did not do to you and/or for you. You did not choose your caregivers! You did not choose their unhealthy ways of treating you. Today, as an adult, you have choices. You do not need to submit to psychological (emotional), physical, mental, social, sexual, or spiritual abuse. You do not need to be controlled by others or try to please others. You have been given a brain that allows you to think, to make choices, and to do what is best for you within your belief system.

If you are being abused in any way by your partner, then you can choose to get help from a safe place or person. This will not be easy, as trauma bonds even in marriages are stronger than normal healthy bonds. You do not need to submit to abuse! There is a better life without it! If this is an issue in your life, you need to take a serious look at the broken boundaries and learn how to set healthy boundaries around your relationship(s). Today, I choose to not submit to others in unhealthy ways.

Day 28 My continued change

The reality is you continue to respond to new situations in the same way you responded in the moment to past trauma. While that was the best response in the past situation, now life is moving forward and often the response from the past is not appropriate to repeat. Practicing breathing, using the correct posture, and grounding are the first steps in the right direction. Beyond this, practice the different responses for the different types of trauma (fight, flight, freeze, and submit) that apply to you. This is not something that changes in a day. It takes a long time to make these kinds of changes. So, keep practicing. Today, I will continue to make small changes in the way that I respond to frustration, anger, and difficult situations.

Healing Relational Trauma

Day 29 Core beliefs

Relationships start early in life. Trauma in a relationship can start at any time. It occurs when our needs are not being met in relationship with another person, especially when we are very young. For example, our needs are not met if our caregiver is somehow unable or unwilling to develop a healthy attachment with us. As a result, we develop negative beliefs about ourselves: "I am worthless, I am helpless, and I am unlovable." This happens whether we are an infant, child, adolescent, or adult when the trauma occurred. These are the deep-seated beliefs that come out in many different ways in life. Today, I will reflect on my core beliefs.

Day 30 Secure attachment

In a secure attachment, the caregiver and the child bond to each other. The child's needs are met. There is contact through the eyes of the caregiver that develops trust in the infant during the first two years of life. This is healthy and desirable. As a result, the child grows up believing in himself or herself. There may be times when all of the child's needs are not met. When this happens, it's more important to repair the harm than it is to actually meet the particular needs. Here the caregiver might say, "I am so sorry; let's go and do something fun together."

Day 31 Avoidant attachment

In avoidant attachment, you simply avoid whatever is going on in your life. This could be in relationships or in responsibilities. At such times, it's essential to take more interest in life, to no longer ignore situations that are unpleasant, taking responsibility for what happens in life, and being responsible for showing up when meeting others. Today, I will be more engaged in my life.

Day 32 Ambivalent attachment

In an ambivalent attachment, you don't care about or take an interest in what happens to your relationships. If you are ambivalent in this way, then you have choices to make in your life. You need to be serious about your relationships. If the other person involved is not someone you want to spend a lot of time with, then you need to make a decision to spend less time with that person. If you value the relationship, then you can choose to spend more time with the person. Today, I will choose my relationships and be more committed to the ones I want.

Day 33 Disorganized attachment

In disorganized attachment, you do not know what to expect from the other person. How will they respond? Will they accept you in the moment or push you away? This is where you need to put boundaries around yourself to keep yourself safe. If someone chooses to push you away, this is not the type of person you will talk with when you need support. I will seek support from a person who is safe for me. Today, I will start the process of finding people and relationships for me that are safe—where I will be accepted and cared for and where I can offer the same in return.

Day 34 Developing safe attachments

Regardless of the type of attachment that you developed in your younger years, today you can earn a secure attachment. You can earn such attachments with safe people, people who allow you to be yourself, to have your own feelings, who respect your boundaries, and who are honest with you. By practicing these changes, you can start to have secure relationships. You can also start to have a secure attachment with yourself by being non-judgmental with yourself and practicing saying, "I am lovable, I am worthwhile, and I am helpful." Today, I will begin to seek secure attachments with others and myself.

Boundaries Around Trauma

Day 35 Boundaries

Trauma has a lot to do with broken boundaries. Natural disasters occur when the natural laws of nature are broken. Car accidents happen when the boundaries of the vehicles are broken for whatever reason. Broken personal boundaries happen in child molestation, sexual assault, hitting, kicking, grabbing, punching, and other physical contact. Then, there is the verbal control, mental control, and manipulation that happens—other forms of broken boundaries. These all lead to trauma. Some people react to such trauma and some do not. How we each react has a lot to do with our internal sense of the world. Today, I will watch for broken boundaries in my life.

Day 36 Changing boundaries

Part of healing trauma includes changing the way you do things so that the same type of trauma does not happen again. If it was a car accident, there may be nothing you can do to change; it may be a onetime event. However, if it is manipulation and control, then you can learn to protect yourself and prevent the same thing from repeatedly happening again. If it was something that happened during military service, then you can look to see if there is something you can change. Or, if it was some type of physical or sexual abuse, then you can learn to put boundaries around it. This would mean learning to say, "Please do not do that." Another boundary may be simply leaving the scene. I will practice setting boundaries.

Day 37 Saying "yes" or "no"

The thing with trauma is that you get stuck in a pattern of using your survival strategies in everyday life situations. So, if the way you dealt with childhood trauma was to submit, then the most likely way you deal with life in general is to submit. This is where learning about boundaries comes into play. Learning to say either "yes" or "no" to anything is extremely important. Perhaps as a young child, you were not allowed to say "yes" or "no." Or maybe saying those words were not taken seriously, so they had no meaning. Saying "yes" or "no" is a boundary. It is letting others know what you will and will not do. Today, I will practice saying "no" and meaning it.

Day 38 Changing hypervigilance

Our bodies become vigilant after abuse—especially physical, emotional, and sexual abuse. The subconscious is always watching for trauma to the point that it is over-reactive in finding trauma. It may be a smell or color of something related to the trauma that you react to. This is normal. The idea is to let it happen, not feel guilty about it. As soon as the conscious kicks in, you can say to yourself, "I am safe because... I am in a different place... I am with different people... My abuser is not here... Nothing harmful is happening to me in this moment, etc." This allows the brain to calm and the emotions to calm down. Today, I will practice telling myself why I am no longer in a traumatic event.

Day 39 Nightmares

Nightmares are a common occurrence with some trauma, though sometimes they do not start until years after the trauma. When a nightmare happens, it is especially scary. If you have been sleeping and are alone, then you can try turning over onto your stomach. This will bring about deep breathing, which will calm down your system. If someone safe is with you and is willing, then you might want to cuddle or talk about it. Or, consider journaling about it to get the thoughts out of your mind and help make some sense of them. If you are journaling and need to make sure no one will read what you wrote, you can always shred the paper when you are done or burn it in a safe place. Today, I will try journaling to see how my thoughts come out on paper and to release some of my negative thoughts.

Day 40 Determining my boundaries

Boundaries need to start from within your soul. You are a unique person! You get to decide how to answer the big questions about yourself, questions like "Who am I?" "Who do I want to become?" "What do I like?" "Who do I want to associate with?" "What hobbies do I want to develop?" "How do I want to treat myself?" "How do I want to treat others?" and "How will I allow others to treat me?" The list goes on. Your internal world and your self-talk are things you get to decide. You also get to choose how you want to react emotionally to others and how you want to go down that path with others. These are all your choices. Today, I will practice making my choices.

Boundaries of Forgiveness (Letting Go)

Day 41 Meaning of forgiveness (letting go)

Forgiveness is for me; it is a letting go of the frustration, the anger, and the resentment that winds around in my head (the thoughts that I cannot stop) after I have been hurt in a big, little, chronic, or complex trauma. Forgiveness is what allows me to start the healing process. It allows the brain chemistry in my head to change. It also allows for more peace and serenity to come into my life.

Forgiveness is not saying "I am sorry" when there is still hatred and anger in my soul. It is not making my children say to one another "I am sorry" when they are not ready. Forgiveness comes from the heart, from the emotional part of my being, from my right brain, and it truly is a letting go of strong emotions. Today, I will begin the process of forgiveness for me.

Day 42 Forgiveness and false guilt

False guilt is when you feel guilt for something that you have not done. There is no need to forgive anyone but yourself for the false guilt. False guilt is what the victim of sexual abuse may feel. Remember, a victim is never guilty. It is also false guilt that you feel when you are controlled or manipulated. This happens when the other person has led you to feel false guilt to make themselves feel better—to be one up on you. It's important to have a safe person to talk with who can help you see that you are not guilty and that you need to forgive yourself and learn to believe in yourself. Today, I will learn to distinguish between false guilt and real guilt. I will also be compassionate in forgiving myself.

Day 43 Seeking forgiveness

The act of seeking forgiveness from another person needs to happen in a protective environment; all parties need to be safe.

When seeking forgiveness, do not expect the other person to be nice about it. He or she may accept the apology and life will go on as before. On the other hand, the other person might respond somewhere else along the possible spectrum of responses—all the way from getting mad and angry to denying that the event ever happened. You need to be prepared for all reactions when seeking forgiveness from another person. Today, I will be intentional about seeking forgiveness in a safe environment.

Day 44 Consequences of forgiveness (consequences, legal issues, and forgetting)

When a person is forgiven, it does not mean that he or she does not need to endure the consequences for the action or inaction. Natural consequences happen all the time. For example, those who decide to jump from a building will suffer the consequence of their action due to gravity, and that could include death. Each country's legal system is another form of consequences. Even if a perpetrator is forgiven by his or her victim, it does not mean that the person does not have to suffer the consequences of the law.

Forgiveness does not mean that the victim

forgets what happened or acts as if it did not happen. After all, the victim needs to be safe! If victims forget, they cannot take the precautionary steps to keep themselves and those around them safe in the future. What forgiveness does mean is that one has released the strong emotions and now can have compassion for the other person while still being safe. Today, I will keep my child(ren) and myself safe.

Day 45 Reconciliation and restitution or forgiveness

Forgiveness does not mean reconciliation. For example, if someone raped me, then it may not be safe to see that person ever again. In fact, I may be putting myself or others in danger by doing so. With any kind of letting go, the event determines if there is any possibility of reconciliation. Where there is physical assault, sexual assault, verbal abuse, or emotional abuse, it is not safe for the partner and the child(ren) to return until the person has undergone treatment and has made a major change in his or her life.

Restitution is where the person who committed the misdeed or offense makes up for what he or she has done wrong. This might mean, for example, replacing something that was taken. It does not, however, guarantee forgiveness—nor does forgiveness mean restitution. The act of forgiving is strictly the choice of the person who was harmed or who harmed. And, in some cases, the legal system determines what is to be given for restitution. It's important to remember that restitution does not always occur. It saves a lot of frustration for the victim to not expect it. Today, I will start the process of forgiving and still keep the other person accountable for his or her actions.

Day 46 Gratitude of forgiveness

It is really hard to grasp the concept that in our affliction, trials, testing, disappointments, and frustrations lies our greatest strength. Certainly, when a trauma happens, it seems there is nothing to be grateful for. Yet, there does come a point after forgiveness (letting go) that you feel gratitude for what has transpired. This is not gladness for the event, but rather gladness for the resulting change that happened in your life. Is does not mean that you will forget the painful event or that when you are reminded of it you will always focus on the positives or have gratitude for it. It means that at some point in time, you will find gratitude for the situation that happened. Today, I choose to find gratitude in my life.

Ways to Help Diminish or Prevent Trauma

Day 47 Mind-body connection

The mind-body connection is now well understood in science. If the body is feeling down and not functioning at peak performance, then it is hard for the mind to function at its peak either. If you are feeling unwell in your body, then it is hard to treat those around you or yourself with respect. You are more likely to get angry or turn to addictions or other sources of coping. Today, I will watch for the mind-body connection.

Day 48 Exercise

Exercise is a great mood stabilizer. I do not remember what I was angry about, but I remember that after I was on the ski hill for an hour, my mood changed and I was no longer angry. Having a regular exercise program (you may need to see your doctor before you start one) helps stabilize your emotions—the lows are not so low, and the highs of frustration, anger, and outrage are not so high. Life becomes more about living in the zone—the zone of peace, joy, and serenity. Today, I will consider starting and maintaining a regular exercise program. Even just walking is acceptable and is all that is needed.

Day 49 Water

Water is what we are mostly made up of. Without it, the body does not get flushed out; the waste products do not get removed as they should. Our brains cannot function at their maximum capacity without water. Our kidneys are more likely to develop kidney stones. And so the list goes on. When you do not drink enough, you are more likely to feel fatigued. Six to eight glasses of water a day have long been the standard recommendation. Today, I will review how much water I am drinking and try to drink enough.

Day 50 Healthful diet

The old saying that you are what you eat is still true. If you eat a lot of sugar and fatty foods, then you are probably not meeting all the nutrient requirements for your body and you're more likely to experience blood sugar on the low side, which makes it more difficult to think clearly. When this happens, you're more likely to do something that you may later regret. Eating regular meals with healthy food helps to prevent mood swings. I will be aware and intentional of what foods I put in my body.

Day 51 Rest

No matter who you are, you still need a good night's sleep to function well. When you are tired, you are more likely to have a hard time doing what you need to do. Plus, it's more difficult to experience the same joy and pleasure that you feel when you are well rested. If you have issues with sleep during the night or you work late, then you can try to take a catnap during the day. Being in the creative zone requires a balance between sleep and energy, especially if you struggle with low blood sugar. What can you do to ensure that you get enough sleep? Today, I will arrange my schedule so that I can get enough sleep to function at my peak potential.

Day 52 Sunshine

Being outside in the sun does something good for the soul. It is hard to describe the effect that it has. Then, there is the vitamin D that you receive from being in the sun. When I am out in nature with my camera, something happens that I cannot describe. My soul somehow fills with joy and happiness. Getting that awesome picture, being in the right place at the right moment, is rewarding. You don't have to be in direct sunlight to get joy from the sun. After all, in this day and age, we need to protect ourselves from getting skin cancer. Even if you're inside looking out into nature (even the sky), you can still benefit from seeing a bright world. Today, I will try to spend time outdoors or otherwise enjoying the sun.

Day 53 Pure air

The quality of air varies in so many places. It's not always possible to get pure, fresh air.

While cities are usually not the best place to find fresh air, indoor air can be just as polluted. It helps to have a carbon filter in the house. Certain plants improve air quality too. Or, you can choose to give your body a break and go to a place where the air quality is better. Today, I will seek the best air quality for my health.

Day 54 Abstinence

Everything around you in your life can be healthy, yet drugs (prescription, nonprescription, and illegal drugs) and other substances could be dulling your mind. Or, you could be struggling with a process addiction like food, sex, love, work, or gambling; these affect the mind in a different way. Any type of addiction makes it harder to be proactive and put boundaries around trauma that may happen. Today, I choose to avoid harmful substances and practices.

Day 55 Spirituality

Spirituality is about a relationship with a Higher Power or God. This does not necessarily have anything to do with following a religious practice. This is about a relationship. If you develop an addiction, it is a way to avoid—to not be intimate with self, others, or God. The practice of spirituality can start with meditation—a way of learning to be by yourself—to avoid the negative self-talk that fills your mind and to just let the thoughts come without judgment. This allows for the calming of the mind and allows your inner voice to be heard—to give direction—so you can find your purpose in life. Today, I will find the time to listen to my inner voice.

Day 56 Emotions

You can also be proactive with your emotions to prevent trauma. Usually your emotions come from your reaction to an event(s) or interpretation of an event(s). You can look at the complete perspective of an event(s) before you decide how you will react emotionally. This means you avoid rationalizing, minimizing, blaming, manipulating, crazy making, and other distracting issues. Another part of this is to allow yourself to hear the positive comments that others are saying about you. This will allow more joy, peace, serenity, and happiness in your life. Today, I will work on controlling my emotions by doing a complete assessment of a situation.

Day 57 Proactive

Being proactive in preventing trauma may be new to you. Really this is all about being the healthiest that you can be regardless of your physical body, your genetics, or your emotions. This prevention allows you to be at your best so you can better deal with trauma or even frustrations that come up. Recently, I was having a phone conversation and I was getting frustrated. In reviewing the conversation later, I concluded that the other person was not listening to what I was saying. She was crossing my boundaries and subtly indicating that I was lying. When I realized this, I was able to let go of the frustration since I understood that the other person had issues. Today, I will do my best to be proactive so I can decrease the effects of future trauma.

Conclusion

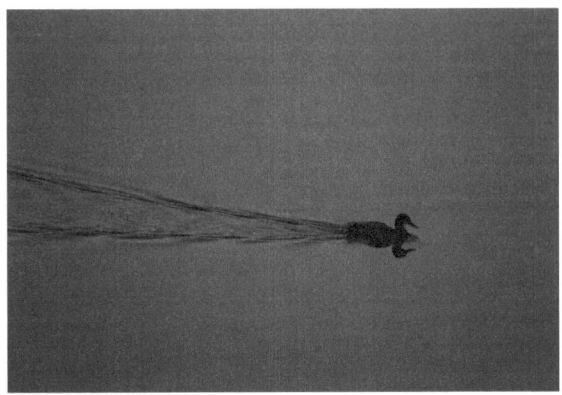

Day 58 Understanding trauma

You have been on an awesome journey over the last fifty-seven days. Congratulations! You have made it to this point in time. There is still a lot of practice to do as you continue to heal from the trauma of the past and work to prevent or deal with trauma and frustration of the future. I encourage you to keep moving forward on this path!

Day 59 What's next?

This is only part of the process of healing trauma. If you have more trauma to heal, you may want to continue to work with the trauma. If you are satisfied with the point you have reached with healing your trauma for now, then there is other work to do—like learning to believe in yourself, trusting yourself, showing yourself respect, not critically judging yourself, loving yourself, and having gratitude for yourself so that you can heal in other ways. These are some of the other areas that you may need to focus on in your life.

Day 60 Continuing on the process

If you have gained only a few of these techniques and have been successful in incorporating them into your life, then you have gained incredible insights. Now you know how to continue the process of dramatically healing from your trauma. May you continue to grow and change into the person you want to be and were meant to be. You are a resilient person, an awesome person! May peace and serenity ever be a part of your life!

Reflective Meditations
Letting Go—Forgiveness

Photography and Script
By Audrey Tait, MS

Contents

1. Introduction.....97
2. Letting Go.....98
3. Letting Go—Forgiveness.....100
4. Broken Boundaries.....103
5. Understanding Emotional Reactions.....107
6. What Is Letting Go?.....110
7. What Letting Go Is Not.....113
8. False Guilt.....116
9. Boundaries in Letting Go.....120
10. Consequences in Letting Go.....123
11. Reconciliation in Letting Go.....126
12. Restitution (Restoration) in Letting Go.....130
13. Gratitude in Letting Go.....133
14. Where to Go from Here.....137

Introduction

Lots of people talk about boundaries. At the end of the day, it is me who has to decide what my boundaries are or what they are going to be. In the past, I may not have been aware of my boundaries. Others may have overstepped my boundaries and I didn't even know it. Anger that comes from within me is my response to someone else breaking my boundaries. Again, I may not even be aware that my boundaries have been broken or what my boundaries are; nonetheless, the boundaries were still there—even unspoken. Right now, my boundaries may be too rigid or too loose. Learning more about boundaries is what this book is all about; learning to have flexible boundaries as needed is the goal. This book is in a meditative format, where one meditation can be read each day—taking the time to think about the idea and reflecting on and making changes as needed. Come with me on this journey of learning and discovery about personal boundaries.

Letting Go

Day 1 Misunderstanding of forgiveness

Forgiveness (letting go) is something that is often misunderstood in our culture. It is the parents saying to their kids, "Say sorry to your brother," when the child is still very emotional over what has happened. It is the victim thinking that he or she has caused the abuse and then living with the resulting false guilt, not knowing it is false guilt. It is also the thinking that one has to forgive when there is no boundary violation. These are all wrong reasons for letting go.

Day 2 Forgiveness is

Forgiveness really is a release of my emotions for me—for my healing. It allows me to move on in life to find serenity and peace and joy and healing. There still needs to be boundaries and consequences of actions; these do not change. Forgiveness is letting go without the need for restitution and reconciliation, as these are the boundary choices of the perpetrator.

Day 3 Come with me on this journey!

Come with me on this journey as we take a more in-depth look at forgiveness. This is a journey that will bring understanding and, if you choose, will start the healing process of releasing your own emotions that keep you trapped and stuck. As we continue this journey, the words "letting go" and "forgiveness" are used interchangeably.

Letting Go—Forgiveness

Day 4 Forgiveness

The question that many ask in life is, "What is forgiveness, and what is letting go?" Understanding forgiveness is important to our healing. Forgiveness is for the person who forgives. It is an emotional release. This does not come easy.... It means letting go of the emotional turmoil in your life, so that you are not trapped and bound by it. It is a new freedom that you get to know, a peace and serenity in your life. This is something that is awesome but takes time to develop. It becomes a state of mind that you live in— peace, serenity, and happiness.

Day 5 Forgiveness of self

Forgiveness of self is for the things I have done that hurt myself. This includes the negative thoughts that keep going around in my head: "I am worthless, I am helpless, and I am unlovable." For the abuse that I may do to my own body, for the neglect of care, for the lack of self-care, for the lack of love for self, lack of gratitude for self, and the list goes on.... This is a private forgiveness.

Day 6 Forgiveness of others

Forgiveness of others is for what they have done to me—the hurt that I have endured from them. Those who have hurt me may include my parents, partner, children, friends, and others. Forgiveness allows me to release (let go) my negative thoughts and hatred toward them. This type of forgiveness or letting go is an emotional release for me. This forgiveness may or may not involve contacting the other person. If the other person is involved, it may be one-on-one or public—but for it to happen, the location needs to be a safe place. If it is not safe for me and/or the other person, then this type of forgiveness should not include the other person. Even if I do not involve or tell the other person involved, this forgiveness still allows me to release the emotional negative thoughts that go around in my head and keep me from healing.

Day 7 Forgiveness of a Higher Power

For those who believe in a Higher Power (or the God of your understanding), at times there is a need for forgiveness or letting to. This again is done for the emotional release that comes. This release brings peace and serenity in life. It is an awesome moment when this happens.

Day 8 Broken boundaries

Letting go or forgiveness is needed when a person has broken boundaries (your boundaries broken by others or others' boundaries broken by you). When no boundaries have been broken, there is no need for forgiveness. At first, this may seem really strange. But it is the same way with problems. If no problem exists, then there is no need to fix it—no need for a new solution. So it is with forgiveness. If there is no break in the relationship—no broken boundaries— there is no need to fix it

Broken Boundaries

Day 9 What boundaries are

Boundaries are all around us. The world has laws that govern it; when these break, we have natural disasters like floods, hurricanes, and earthquakes. Along with this, we have gravity, the speed of sound, rules of flight, and so on. For me personally, I have boundaries although I may not know it. My skin is the outer boundary of my body; inside my body are boundaries between every cell. Between us and other people there are boundaries. I have social, physical, psychological, intellectual, sexual, and spiritual boundaries. Many of these boundaries are based on my beliefs about myself. You can find more information on boundaries in my book Reflective Meditations: Understanding My Boundaries, *available at Amazon.*

Day 10 What broken boundaries are

Broken boundaries occur when the space around me has been violated. This may be a breaking of my personal, social, intellectual, physical, psychological, sexual, or spiritual boundaries. Socially, someone may have not fulfilled a commitment to a social engagement, has not shown up or called. Physically, my body may have been damaged; I may have been punched, grabbed, pulled, or seriously hurt by an assault. Sexually, I may have been assaulted or raped, or I could have been harmed by negative sexual comments that others said about me. Intellectually, I may have experienced put-downs or have endured a physical assault on the brain that affects my intellect. Spiritual boundaries may have been broken when others manipulated and/or controlled me to follow their own beliefs. Psychologically, boundaries may break if others do not allow me to have emotions for an extended time; it could be the young child who is always told to stop crying or the adult who is somehow not allowed to express his or her feelings. These are all forms of broken boundaries.

Day 11 My reactions to broken boundaries

There are two basic reactions to broken boundaries. There are those who spray like a skunk—who blame others when they are at fault. This may bring some relief in the moment for the "sprayers," but it is not a long-term solution. Addicts often react this way. Then, there are those individuals who are sprayed at and take it in like a turtle. This reaction keeps the feelings on the inside and the person mentally chews it over and over again. Reacting in this way leads to stuffed anger and possible depression. Both types of reactions to broken boundaries have a real emotional element and consequences. These are unhealthy ways of dealing with broken boundaries. Being assertive and stating what I need is a healthy way to deal with boundary violations.

Day 12 Denial as a broken boundary

Denial is an unhealthy way of dealing with broken boundaries. In denial, you stuff down what has happened, try to forget it, avoid the emotions connected to what happened, and strive to prevent others from knowing what happened. This is the keeping of family secrets that are so devastating. If you are in denial, you do not allow the healing to happen, nor do you work through the broken boundaries, abuse, and trauma. You also deny yourself a better life during and after healing.

Day 13 Trauma as a broken boundary

Trauma is a broken boundary. It is the type of offense that is more devastating than other boundary violations. Trauma occurs with car accidents, sexual assault or rape, natural disasters, military service, and the list goes on. It is common to experience emotional reactions from trauma. This is different for everyone. The reaction has a lot to do with how secure the individuals are with themselves and those around them, as well as how much support they have for dealing with the issues.

Understanding Emotional Reactions

Day 14 Anger

Anger and all its forms—from frustration to aggression to rage—stems from a broken boundary. Somebody has done something that you do not like, and you have reacted to it emotionally. There is nothing wrong with anger. The problem comes with the way that you deal with the anger. Anger can be seen in the outward aggression that is expressed against another. Then there is the inward aggression of self-harm, including suicide.

Day 15 Addictions

Addiction is another emotional response to trauma. The person turns to a substance or process rather than face what has happened.

It is a form of denial. To avoid the emotional reaction that stems from the original situation, the person just leaves it behind and hides behind substance addictions, process addictions, compulsive attachments, and feelings. Narcissistic (self-absorbed) traits and unhealthy ways of dealing with emotions can also occur, making others feel guilty for the person's issues and for not connecting with life.

Day 16 Fear/terror

Fear or terror is another response to trauma. When this happens, the response can become a way of life and you are never comfortable around yourself and others. The body is always looking for fearful situations. It is hard to relax. It takes concentrated effort to learn to face your fears in a healthy environment.

Day 17 Depression

Another emotional response to trauma is depression, which is a form of repressed anger. In this case, the depression is really anger that was not dealt with in a healthy way. In fact, the anger was not really dealt with at all and that has led to depression. The person feels extremely low or down as a result of not dealing with what is going on in life. It will take concerted effort to get going again. You'll need to learn about boundaries and what you will put up with and will not put up with. To back up the boundaries, you will need to set consequences that you are willing to follow through with.

Day 18 My way of responding

It is wise to learn what your emotional reactions are to broken boundaries, as we tend to respond in the same way most of the time. You can track this for a number of weeks and see what is happening in your life. Doing so helps you find the problem so that you can deal with the issues and start the process of letting go. Unless you know the issues, it is hard to let go of the emotions around forgiveness.

What Is Letting Go?

Day 19 Letting go

Letting go (forgiveness) is for me. It is the release of the strong emotions I have felt in response to breaking my own boundaries or other people breaking my boundaries. Some small breaches in a relationship are easy to let go. Others are more serious and may call for boundaries and consequences. Still others are so significant that I must remove myself from the situation and may never see that person again. Safety is paramount in all my relationships—even in letting go.

Day 20 Releasing strong emotions

There are things I can do to help release those strong emotions in order to move forward in life and to not be stuck in those emotions. This will depend on how I best deal with my emotions—it may be by myself, in the privacy of my home, or it may be with others who are safe and are willing to listen to me. How do I best deal with my strong emotions?

Day 21 Dealing with emotions by oneself

When I need to deal with strong emotions and I am by myself, I can breathe through my diaphragm, stand up, or lie down on my stomach. These strategies will help me breathe deeply and allow my system to relax. Then, there is journaling that puts my thoughts on paper (this can be shredded if I do not want someone else to read my thoughts). The process of naming an event gets the left and right sides of my brain involved in the calming process.

Day 22 Dealing with strong emotions with others

When I am around safe people, I may be able to talk over the matter with someone else. This allows my emotions to begin defusing. I may need to discuss the issue many times. If it is something deep that has been around for a long time, then I may need to seek professional counseling to help me move through the process and build a better life.

Day 23 Prevention

There are things I can do to prevent getting in a situation where I will have strong emotions. I may need to avoid certain people or places. Exercise is a great mood stabilizer; it helps my emotions from escalating to the extremes. A regular exercise program can help me regulate my emotions. Eating a proper diet prevents me from getting low blood sugar and getting frustrated so easily. Drinking enough water helps me avoid being fatigued and enables me to better deal with life. There are many other ways to regulate my emotions so I can focus on living life with more serenity, peace, and happiness.

What Letting Go Is Not

Day 24 Boundaries

Letting go is a boundary issue. I can let go of the hurt, anger, and pent-up feeling(s) I have—to find release for me. That is what forgiveness is. I will remember that forgiveness is for me; it has nothing to do with the other person. Forgiveness is not controlling, manipulating, or abusing the other person to change.

Day 25 Letting go is not

Forgiveness is not saying, "I am sorry" when my heart, mind, and soul are saying, "I still have issues around this. I still feel hurt, I still believe the other person is at fault, I still want the other person punished, and I still want him or her to say, 'I was wrong, I forgive you, and I will do this to make it up to you.'" What the other person does is his or her decision. I cannot force, manipulate, or control the other person to do as I wish. That is not my choice. That is the boundary issue.

Day 26 Letting go is not telling everything

Forgiveness does not mean that you are free to tell all the juicy details around the grapevine in your environment of family, friends, colleagues, and/or others. Although you may need to name the event to keep others safe, beyond that, none of the details need to be shared. This is also what happens in a disclosure between partners. Although, for example, the partner needs to know that this person had a sexual relationship with ten other people, the disclosure does not include all of the juicy details. Rather, it allows the truth to be told so the other partner knows what he or she needs to know —so that person can plan and determine what he or she will tolerate and will not tolerate. It also gives enough information to help the person decide whether to stay or leave. The partner also knows to get tested for sexually transmitted diseases.

Day 27 Letting go in not about hurting the other person

Letting go is not about hurting the other person. At times, you may want to see the other person hurt, to suffer for his or her actions. This is not part of letting go. Letting go, releases or lets go of the feelings that have been spinning around in your head. When you have let go of the strong emotions, then you no longer want to see the other person hurt—you may even develop empathy toward the person. This, however, does not mean that there are no boundaries, consequences, or reporting of the other person.

False Guilt

Day 28 False guilt

Victims often carry false guilt related to traumatic events. And perpetrators want their victims to feel at fault. They may try to make their victims feel this way by saying things like, "Don't tell anyone or I will kill you," "You caused me to do that to you," "It's all your fault," or "You deserved it for what you did." And so the list goes on. ***The victim is never guilty—never, never, never guilty!***

Day 29 My false guilt

I may be allowing myself to feel false guilt. This is the false statement(s) that I say to myself and allow to take over my mind. It is versions of the core beliefs that "I am helpless," "I am worthless," and "I am unlovable." These statements can be less intense and sound like "I can never do that," "I am not worthy to have that item," and "This person will never love me if he or she really knows me." I need to realize that this is false guilt. Then I need to let go of these statements and replace them with positive statements like "I am helpful," "I am lovable," and "I am worthwhile."

Day 30 Other's false guilt

Then, there is the other kind of false guilt that develops when someone else tries to make me feel at fault. This happens in manipulation, control, and/or abuse. The other person is trying to make me feel responsible for what is happening. They do this in an effort to make themselves feel better. In reality, it is not my fault. I do not need to accept their statements as true. I need to understand that they are acting as they did in the past, and I need to let go of my own emotional reaction to what they are doing. I may need to put boundaries and consequences around them, so I do not repeatedly feel the same way.

Day 31 Victim's false guilt

Then there are the extreme cases of abuse and trauma. The words said in such situations are always meant to produce false guilt. For example, the abuser of a child may say, "Don't tell anyone about our special relationship or I will kill you." In my case, the words were said years later: "You do not want to take it to court; it will only ruin your little ones." What a lie! My reaction to the trauma hurt my children in the ways that I dealt with them in everyday life. If you have been abused, seek treatment today so that you can understand that the victim in never guilty. **I will say it again: the victim is never guilty—the victim only feels false guilt.**

Day 32 Changing false guilt

I do not need to suffer from false guilt. I can determine that I should not feel guilty. This may mean talking with other safe people; it may be something that I can determine on my own. It may mean being completely honest with myself, finding the meaning behind what has happened, and looking at it from different perspectives. Then, it is a matter of letting go of the feelings around what has happened. There may need to be boundaries and consequences so that the same scenario does not get repeated again and again.

Boundaries in Letting Go

Day 33 Boundary issues

Forgiveness is a boundary issue. I can forgive myself, I can forgive the other person, and I can ask for my Higher Power's forgiveness. I cannot expect any of this from the other person. If I go to the other person to seek reconciliation and restitution, I must be prepared for the person to react in any number of ways—anything from being calm and peaceful to saying he or she never wants to see me again to exploding in my face, causing me more trauma. The person could even deny that the event happened. Safety is always paramount!

Day 34 Boundaries around the perpetrator

Forgiveness (letting go) is a boundary issue. Forgiveness is for me; it is letting go of the strong emotions that keep me bound up and tied up in my mind. It allows me to seek peace, serenity, and joy in my life, to allow my body to calm down from my reactions. I cannot change the other person; that is only something that he or she can do. That is why forgiveness is a boundary issue. If I try to change the other person, then I am manipulating, controlling, and/or abusing him or her.

Day 35 Boundaries around manipulation and control

Others may have no boundaries around forgiveness. They may continue to try to manipulate and control me. This is where I need to create boundaries around myself, to keep myself and/or my dependent(s) safe. If the boundaries do not work through discussion, then I need to set consequences that will back up my boundaries and convince the other person that I mean business. If this does not work or has not worked in the past, I may need to remove myself and/or my dependent(s) from the situation. This is the boundary issue of forgiveness.

Day 36 Boundaries around abuse

When abuse has occurred, I may need to take immediate action to remove myself and/or my dependent(s) from the situation. This is a safety boundary. This is where others need to suffer the consequences of their actions. I do not turn around and say, "That was okay; I forgive you and forget about it." Doing so would be to deny the reality of the situation; this does not keep myself safe in the future.

Day 37 Boundaries of my own needs

Another area of boundaries is those around myself. These involve self-care issues, such as taking care of myself first and looking after my body and keeping it healthy. I also look after my social, physical, psychological, intellectual, sexual, and spiritual needs. This is like the airplane mask when flying. If the oxygen level goes low, I need to put on my own oxygen mask before helping someone else with their mask. So, in life I must take care of my own needs first, even before those of my children.

Consequences in Letting Go

Day 38 Consequences

Forgiving someone does not mean the person will not have to suffer the consequence(s) of the action. There has been a breach of the relationship. The consequence may be something simple that is later forgotten over the years, or it may be complex and affect the relationship for all time.

Day 39 Experiencing consequences does not mean forgetting

I do not forget what happened just because the person experienced consequence(s). The trauma of the event is still there. For example, victims of sexual violations, like child molestation, sexual assault, and rape, still carry the memory of the event and the resulting trauma even if the perpetrator was imprisoned. The memories remain and current events will still remind the victim of the trauma. Even when you think there is nothing else to heal about the event, certain events or situations may trigger memories of the trauma. This will happen even when there has been forgiveness and a settling of the matter—even legally.

Day 40 Separation consequences

In a relationship, partners need to set boundaries around what they will and will not tolerate. This makes for a healthy relationship. If abuse occurs in the relationship, there needs to be boundaries and consequences. If that does not change the behavior, then you may need to leave for the sake of being safe. Safety is always paramount in a partner relationship. If you are to return to the relationship, this needs to be done in a safe manner. It takes time to build trust again. It's important to avoid blind trust—where there are no action(s) to support what is being said by the partner

Day 41 Legal consequences

Broken boundaries may involve legal consequences, and I may need to report the boundary violation. In this case, if someone else does not report what happens, then I need to do the right thing and report it. This may be the hardest thing I have ever done. It may mean feeling unsafe and needing protection by the law. I will need to get all the help I can during the process of doing what needs to be done. My dependent(s) and I are worth being treated with justice.

Day 42 Boundaries for the perpetrator

Forgiveness does not mean that the perpetrator is free to do as he or she wants. There should be boundaries put around this person. If this is a legal case, then it needs to be reported according to your local laws. If children have been hurt sexually, then the perpetrator should never be left alone with children. Remember, boundaries are essential to the safety of many.

Reconciliation in Letting Go

Day 43 Reconciliation

Forgiveness is about the release of my emotions that go round and round in my head. When I forgive, I let go of these emotions. Forgiveness does not mean, however, that I let go of boundaries or that I will reconcile with the other person. These are distinctly different actions.

Day 44 Reconciliation and forgiveness

Reconciliation may or may not happen when I let go and forgive. To reconcile means to reconnect in the relationship, to return to the point where it was before. Whether or not this happens depends on the particular situation. If it was a misunderstanding that has been discussed and resolved, then reconciliation may be possible—the situation will go back to normal or close to normal.

Reconciliation does not mean that you forget what happened. If the offense happens repeatedly, then you need to set boundaries around it and follow the boundaries with consequences. For example, if the person continues to miss appointments, then I will make it clear that I will not tolerate this; I will follow up this boundary with the consequence of not seeing the person for two weeks.

Day 45 Partner relationships

Partner relationships can be tricky when it comes to breaking boundaries. There may be minor boundary violations that can be dealt with by talking about it and then making changes. This involves setting up a time to discuss the issue in a non-judgmental way. Here each person gets to explain their side of the issue without the other person interrupting; then the other person gets to respond. If this becomes an emotional discussion, then it's best to take a break and set a time to come back to the topic at a later point.

Day 46 Partner reconciliation in question

In some cases, one partner may need to leave the relationship. If there are children involved and there is a safety issue(s), you need to leave immediately. In time, you may want to return to the relationship; however, it's important to understand that in trauma, a trauma bond has been formed. It is a stronger bond than in a normal partner relationship. It may take time to build up trust that the other person has made significant changes—this usually takes treatment and possibly supervised visitation with the children. Do not rush reconciliation in this type of relationship. Remember that domestic violence has a cycle and, without significant intervention, that cycle keeps repeating and escalating. You will know that you are in a difficult relationship if you are always walking on eggshells and never know what will spark abuse from your partner.

Day 47 Reconciliation and trauma

In any relationship, safety is number one. Sometimes, it will not be safe to heal the relationship. If there has been trauma and abuse that is intolerable, then it needs to be dealt with. If this is rape by a stranger, then reconciliation may never happen. If there are laws that have been broken, then the offense needs to be reported so the justice system can do its job. Your number one job is to keep yourself and your dependent(s) safe.

Restitution (Restoration) in Letting Go

Day 48 What is restitution?

Restitution is an act of replacing what has been taken from the victim. In a car accident, the car insurance works to repair the physical injury and return the body to the place it was before. When my back and neck were hurt in the fourth not-at-fault accident in four years, the idea was to return my body to the way it was before the last car accident. In a house fire, the insurance is intended to repair the house to the way it was before the fire. In sexual assault, it is hard to return the body and mind to where they were before. In such cases, the court may order an amount of money to help the victim progress in life.

Day 49 Restitution is not a right

Again, restitution is an act of replacing what has been taken from the victim. This is not a right of the victim—the victim cannot demand anything from the perpetrator. Certainly, where there is an accident, insurance can replace what was lost. In cases of physical, sexual, and verbal abuse, a court will likely determine restitution. If restitution is available, it may help to solve some of the issues. It does not, however, take away what happened. It does not resolve the feelings, nor does it take away the trauma. There is still suffering.

Day 50 Restitution and the law

Some boundary violations break the law of where you are living. These kinds of incidents need to be reported. This is the right of the victim to report. In some places, professionals are mandated to report certain offenses. This has to be done regardless of forgiveness. These are the type of cases in which the court may determine restitution.

Day 51 Restitution—a difficult issue

This may be one of the hardest things for a

victim to realize: letting go includes releasing the right for restitution. Again, this is a boundary issue. The perpetrator has the right to decide whether or not to give restitution. If this is something that is forced by the victim, then the victim has become the perpetrator in a difference sense—by forcing restitution. This, too, is a boundary issue. Force, manipulation, and control are not part of forgiveness. Forgiveness means letting go of the emotional turmoil within myself.

Gratitude in Letting Go

Day 52 Gratitude

It would seem impossible to have any kind of gratitude for being a victim, whether the offense was something like manipulation and control or outright abuse. At first your emotions may run wild. It may be years before the gratitude comes. Healing trauma is like opening the door a crack at first and then slowly opening it more and more until you can finally swing it open wide. This happens when emotions are not driving your life. At this point, gratitude can start to form. It may not be gratitude for the event that happened, but rather gratitude for the change and growth that occurred in your life.

Day 53 My gratitude

I, as the author of this book, would not be the person I am without the trauma that I have been through. I would not have the academic degrees that I have earned or the extra training that I have been through. My purpose and path would likely be different. Am I glad for the trauma? Not necessarily. Yet I am extremely glad for the healing that has come. This does not mean that I do not have flashbacks about the abuse or that I will ever forget what happened. It just means that I am in a different place than when I was denying the abuse.

Day 54 Brain changes

There are some awesome brain changes that happen when you come to the place of gratitude. Having gratitude is a practice that is essential to bringing more peace, love, and joy into your life. You can practice gratitude by doing something as a part of your daily life. It can be as simple as naming five things that you are grateful for at the end of the day. This practice will allow your brain to change in positive ways for a better healing experience.

Day 55 Gratitude for yourself

Gratitude is also for yourself. You may have gratitude when you have done a good job, made a difficult decision, and followed through on the decision, among many other reasons or accomplishments. Having gratitude for yourself also means ending the negative thoughts about yourself that keep you from peace, love, joy, and serenity in life.

Day 56 Gratitude for others

Expressing gratitude for others lets them know what you like about them. This allows others to have a witness—a fair witness— who helps them see who they truly are. This changes their brain in ways that make it healthier. It also changes your brain. In fact, the mirror neurons in the brain become synced with one another, which improves your relationship. When expressing gratitude to someone else, it's important to be honest—do not say something if it is not true.

Day 57 Receiving gratitude

Having gratitude also means being able to receive gratitude from another person. It is saying "thank you" without explaining away what the other person has said. It is not rationalizing away the comment when the other person is not around. It is truly receiving gratitude from the other person. This allows the other person to experience those awesome brain changes.

Where to Go from Here

Day 58 Summary

Now that we're near the end of this book, you have a better understanding of forgiveness. It is about you—letting go of those feelings that keep spinning around in your head and that you seem unable to stop. It is not allowing false guilt to take possession of you. It is forgiving yourself and others. Forgiveness does not want revenge on the other person. Along with this are the boundaries and consequences that you set around manipulation, control, and abuse. You do not have the right to receive restitution and reconciliation, as these are the perpetrator's boundaries. However, a court might order restitution.

Day 59 Starting to change

I can start to change today by admitting the abuse that I have gone through and not denying it. I can take the time I need to heal my emotions and release them. This is a process. I can be proactive with boundaries and consequences of abuse, even reporting offenses if I need to. I can start being grateful as a regular practice in my life.

Day 60 Continuation of the journey

This has been an awesome journey of understanding. Thank you for coming on it with me. I, as the author, have developed a better understanding of forgiveness as I have written this book. I have found areas that I need to forgive myself for personally and have started that process. It is all part of my healing journey. As you continue on your own journey, may the peace of the God of your understanding be with you and bring you peace, love, joy, serenity, and happiness.

Further Reading

Reflective Meditations Trilogy:
Understanding My Authentic Self;
Believing in Myself;
Loving Myself;
Plus Understanding My Boundaries
Script and photography by Audrey Tait, MS

I Am Wonderfully Me:
Positive Affirmations for Me!
Volume 1-3
Script and photography by Audrey Tait, MS

About the Author

Audrey Tait has a love of photography and has a master's degree in Addiction Counseling and a bachelor's degree in Dietetics. She is a Canadian Certified Counsellor; Certified Sex Addiction Therapist, candidate; Certified Multiple Addiction Therapist, candidate; and Registered Dietitian, Alberta, Canada. In addition, she is a member of the Canadian Counselling and Psychotherapy Association; College of Dietitians of Alberta; and the Alpha Chi Honors Society. She has specialized training in trauma, character, and developmental issues along with cognitive therapy. She is owner/ president of Inspirational Insights Counselling, Inc., where therapy is offered to those seeking a deeper meaning in life.

www.inspirationalinsightcounselling.com